The Last Regatta

MAURICE HARMON

Salmon Poetry

Published in 2000 by
Salmon Publishing Ltd,
Cliffs of Moher, Co. Clare, Ireland
http://www.salmonpoetry.com
email: info@salmonpoetry.com

A catalogue record for this book is available from the British Library.

The Arts Council
An Chomhairle Ealaíon

Salmon Publishing gratefully acknowledges the financial assistance of The Arts Council/An Chomhairle Ealaíon.

ISBN 1 903392 08 X Paperback

Cover design by Brenda Dermody
Set by Siobhán Hutson
Printed by Techman Ireland Ltd., Dublin

for Maura

Acknowledgements

Acknowledgements are due to the following publications where some of these poems previously appeared:
ABEI Journal, *Books Ireland*, *The Burning Bush*, *Irish University Review*, *Orbis*, *Poetry Ireland Review*.

'In those days, in that place' appeared in *Thistledown. Poems for UNICEF*, edited by John F. Deane, 1990.

'A Stillness at Kiawah' was published in a limited edition by Three Spires Press, 1996.

'Late Summer Lake Nojiri' and 'The Last Regatta' were published in *Poets for the Millenium*, edited by Ian Wild, 1999.

'Ardgillan' and 'Letter to My Daughter' appeared in *Poetry Now Anthology*, edited by Patrick Galvin, 2000.

Contents

Japanese Garden

HILL NORTH BLACK TURTLE THREE CYPRESS

PATH WEST WHITE TIGER SEVEN MAPLES

azaleas pruned to mountain peaks

stones in attitudes

arranged

disarranged

take heart

where two roads cross

and four roads join

black

red

blue

white

STREAM EAST BLUE DRAGON NINE WILLOWS

POND SOUTH CRIMSON BIRD NINE JUDAS

Azaleas

You can see the blossom increase and grow
on the nine azalea bushes in our garden.

Every day the sun shines for hours.
Every other day it rains softly.

Today the bees arrive, flying
from one bush to the next in sweet delight.

But although their backs are beetle shelled,
the crow on the white bush picks them off like flies.

Each day the blooms increase
and each day the black snapper feeds.

Soon not much will be left.
The beautiful pink and white blossom will fall.

The bees will go away.
Only the sacred bird will stay.

Afternoon Tea

We have come a long way for this:
the music building with its vane trumpeter,

the fluent stream, the plenitude of webs
in the low-sized evergreens,

our tea ceremony under the trees
beside the lacecap hydrangeas.

By local lore we do not do it right,
but I love the eager way you bring out

the latest batch of rock buns,
or the plate of hot buttered scones.

The water, you say, must be piping hot,
the pot scalded, the tea drawn.

We've done it this way for years.
I may not sweep the path,

or sprinkle water on stone,
but my heart bows to you.

Figures

In front of me a table rock in three segments
water washes over and drains slowly back
turning water-weed to a satiny sheen.

Out in the bay below a bare perpendicular rock
a solitary flat-bottomed boat with a straw roof
under which a figure sits all morning motionless.

Beyond him tier upon tier of mountain peaks,
line after line, and in between a grey blue mist
suggesting ravines, and winding, upward tracks.

On one of these, under a single tree
with a branch arched to the right, a smudged
distinct shape heading for the next height.

I sit by the water's edge in flow and fall,
the boatman keeps his fixed, unhurried hour,
the mountains rise, imprinted for all time in mist.

Happy here in a daze of contentment,
my mind travels with that other shape,
the mist opening and closing, keeping the space

in which he moves. I could follow that dark shape,
that frail, indomitable form into the night,
the mist opening out, then closing at my back.

Frozen Phoenix

There are moments like that
when the tongue sticks in the throat's bell
never to fall free again.

Never to sound the alarm or the all clear.
The blocking source the frail rigging
of the mosquito net in merciless spasm.

The lift and suck at the mothering core.
Never to be meshed in words,
stopped in mid-gulp.

When the father's dark hands
clapped the eyes across,
his breath hot on his son's neck.

Moments like that warp speech
and words that ought to clear
and cleanse knot in the throat.

from an incident in *The Temple of the Golden Pavilion*
by Yukio Mishimo

Late Summer Lake Nojiri

The dragon flies make tandem flights
steering a straight course, rising
and sinking as the light breeze blows

like a piece of silken thread stretched tight
from end to end, two sets of double wings
so clarified in the slowly sinking light

one cannot see their soft tremulous beat
joined tip to tip in their mating flight
their union is subtly gently held

and steady as they go, no
rapturous heights, no sudden lows
but holding the line as the sun goes

Letter to my Daughter

The cold up north drove them back at us.
They slithered across the path beside our feet,
burst through screens, breaking and entering.

The place so musty we slept on the gallery floor,
conscious of timber racked behind our heads,
of rustling, slitherings along the roof.

Silence stopped me when we came back here.
Sevenday locusts no longer had hysterics,
no longer blundered from the cherry trees.

Spider hammocks sagged like fallen floors
in disused rooms. Sated dragon flies
no longer rode with swallows or with bats.

When you told me your friend was dead,
that was the season's final emptying,
good days drained, cold along the boards.

'complete strangers on this road'

There he was
a decent man travelling
through places
with horrible names:

'children-desert-parents',
'parents-desert-children',
'dog-denying'.
'horse-repelling'.

There they were
two women
on their way
to the Shrine at Ise.

Making love each night
to a different man,
lives like white froth
beating to the strand.

They asked if they might follow
behind,
at a distance.
He made excuses.

from an incident in Matsuo Basho's *The Narrow Road to the Deep North*

The Last Regatta

Beside the tiny pool beside the house
I sometimes pause these late November days
to watch maple leaves flaring down

to clear water and there upheld awhile,
red incorrigible sails that seek and find
the slightest breeze for one final run.

Although no warnings here of gale-force winds
relay the ending of their carefree days
they are sinking slowly, water-logged,

and swirling gently, listing into silt,
minute pyres burning softly down.
It is a good way to go, trim

and tidy as they furl stricken sheets,
tighten lines, prepare for wet dock.
They've had their seasons and their seasons' days,

have hoisted tapestries to catch the breeze,
have known beauty in this temperate place
where a stone lantern keeps constant watch.

They are ending passage now in their own way,
in their own time, untouched by human hand,
unhurried, unshaken, beyond the reach of man.

Shunkan

There was no thought of fighting the waves.
They pulled the ground from under him
and pushed the sea around him, true blue
and streaked with white caps, pushed it
firmly, then sent the entire rock about
until he was fixed in that hard blue,
that desolate cold blue and white.

There was no mention of Troy, he stood
watching the ship's decline.
No sounds now, no stretched cries,
no bird song, no jungle howl, no bent notes.
All the attention in eyes that strained,
scanned, imagining hands,
contracting absence in sunken depths.

There was no question of being tied to the stone.
He clambered there, holding on to a single vine,
desperate, clawed, fought through the one tree,
held down a branch, leaned out, far out,
fell when the branch broke, but groped again upright,
all yearning, sight fading, light going, ship
receding, far off, dimming, away, away.

The part of Shunkan was performed by the Kabuki actor, Kichiemon, at Kyoto's Minamiza Theatre in December 1997

A Stillness at Kiawah

Many of these poems, set in Kiawah, an island off the coast of South Carolina, draw upon native American and Irish mythology and suggest parallels between the history of the Kiowas during the westward advance of an alien civilization and the history of the Irish during a similar experience.

There are many similarities between the mythologies of the small Kiowa tribe and the Irish: in both human ancestors are connected with divinity, people change into birds and animals, and the division between reality and the spirit world is magically erased. In the modern period the Kiowas and the Irish experienced territorial and cultural dispossession.

A Pictured History

i.
These woods
are not my woods
yet what I find here

the history
the myth
I cannot ignore

ii.
a people set
their story down
inscribed the log

of what they know
the gist of things
in toy figures

cartoon shapes
of men and animals
deeds of war

arrows shooting
at heads
inside the barriers

gouts of blood
black dots for disease
symbolic leaves

winter's black bar
white space
for the sun dance

the stab
of greater force
thrusts

that cut their lands
this way that way
when all they had known

was space and sky
the great herds
manners of life and death

iii.

a people
born
from a hollow log

a tree
lifts a child
to the sun

a ring
splits a boy
into two half-boys

a boy
become bear
become water beast

a mole
mouths a circle
of fine earth

stars
driven on the world
like rain

iv.
fighters, stealers,
hunters,
priests of the sun

'insubordinate', 'insolent',
'unmanageable'

v.
ten men
wore the sash
ten men
fixed spears
and stood their ground
ten men knew
go forward meant
go back

vi.
a bad time
they went south
were brought back

were shut up
in the horse corral
all winter long

were let out
when the soldiers' horses
had eaten all the grass

lost their young men
in the fighting
lost their food

when the buffalo went
hung the red blanket
in vain

vii.

Folded bone to bone
under heaving snow
neither doll power
nor spirit prayer
brought them home.

They circled north and west
to throw the teacher off their tracks
had so much craft misled their friends
but did not know the ruffling clouds
would drive flocks of heron down the skies
would turn hills and ridges to ghost herds
pawing the ground, bellowing over the plain
would shred flakes of horn into their eyes
would clog their throats with furry breath.

viii.

the old man
did not speak
when the warriors
rode in with blackened faces

the women wailed
gashed legs and arms
cut off finger tips
piled ashes on their heads
burnt what the dead man owned
until he said

'I want my son with me.
What is left of my son
I want with me.
This is his tipi.
This is his horse.
These are his clothes.
This is where he belongs'.

ix.

Back from the dead
animal tracks
mislead his trackers

women dread his coyote's
dried muzzle
his scabs and scars

his death's head
scraped to the bone

x.

'I live, but not forever
Mysterious moon, you alone remain'

the old warrior sang
like a young man
starting out

'Powerful sun, you alone remain
Wonderful earth, you live forever'

xi.

their dead
took their names with them

built their camp fires
in the Milky Way

carried dreams
in their voices

sang the spirit song

xii.
War Bonnet Sun Dance
Sun Flower Growing Sun Dance
Love-Making Sun Dance
Cholera Sun Dance
Horse-Eating Sun Dance
No Sun Dance
No Sun Dance
No Sun Dance
Sun Dance When the Forked Poles Were Left Standing

xiii.
the noose of greed
pulled tight
year after year

they must cringe
or rebel
either way

the bitter result
elders jailed
weapons horses removed

the sun dance outlawed

these woods not my woods
but here I find
our own defeats

xiv.
After a night
when the storm horse
howled in the sky

and lashed his tail
I walked inland
from a shore

made wild with wreckage
and driftwood
that day she went north

for her father's funeral
a go-getter
with eleven children

each by a different woman
she feared that mustering
of scattered kin

nomads
beyond the sun dance
range

xv.
I seek
a dome shaped
sweat-lodge

heated stones
lashing tails
the fume of dark air

discover a people
born from a hollow log
a pictured history.

The Search

PART 1

i.

I look everywhere, circle water
holes, inspect where a sign says
'alligator pool', malinger

imagine a twitch of snout,
hypnotic gleams
from soft, tumescent eyes

crouch under brush and palm,
sniff dank enclaves,
feel the scratch of Spanish moss

unsure what may slide
out of the depths, nobbly, whelked,
smelling of crotch and crack

night beast I used to dread
heaving toward me with
taut, irreproachable breasts.

ii.

the bank
where you took the sun
was stained

the grass stems
crushed and bloody
I follow a trail

of broken roots
scraped bark
torn earth

my heart hammering
lest you or another
might rear fiercely

out of a pool
with lashing tail
and grid of bared teeth

find you with
raw wounds
along the ridges

of your great head
one whole side
ripped

in a jagged seam
your powerful tail
limp as a wet leaf

iii.

I sensed you
moon-eyed
within the water oaks

when you attacked
your claws
raked my chest

I struck you away
you circled
swept downward

plunged
a fierce, shredding beak
between my teeth

I wrenched free
fell backward
towards the ground

you came again
straddled my thighs
ripped the thin covering

gripped the ridged flesh
ate
straight to the bone

iv.
At almost any time
I find you
motionless

beside a lagoon
or feeding
in a marsh

immaculately white
the silver strings
of your breeding plumes

delicate
as fine rain
as though mud suck

weed cling
the stench of things
leave you untouched

v.
On a bare rock
your neck
writhes

your face shuts
sucks air
fills with sound

strains
from cry
to screech

when I reach out
you twist mutely
back

vi.
your face
fills with light
gently I touch

frail bones
that lift in love
and trust

forgive me
I must knead
bone against bone

flesh against flesh
fill you
with sweat and strain

no other way
but the old way
of ruck and slime

vii.
When I awoke
you were a soft snout
nuzzling my ear

your narrow tongue
damping my temple's
white tufts

while I slept
you padded in
from the trees

risen from some lair
of fern and early leaf
face beaded with dew

now as my mouth
reaches yours
kissing under your lips

a gentle moisture
seeps onto our chins
as kissing deeply

our bodies join
yours redolent
of redwood bark and pine

when you crouch
over me
the morning light

brightens your back
my sitting bear
my beast of the day

PART 2

i.
First the radiance
in the mist
attracted you

then my head and haunches
cleared
and held your gaze

when I turned
and fled
you followed

when I plunged
into the lake
you were near

when I slowed
in a ring
you crossed

a bright loop
that stirred
drawing us close

under your hands
uncertain shapes
dissolving forms

face and hair
water borne
my thighs transfiguring

ii.
I was a salmon
leaping falls
softer than lake water

a brightness
brighter than sunlight
in morning mist

a swiftness
swifter than swallows
in midge swarm

when I surged
up to you
you ate the rowan's

ancient light
from my finger-tips
and drifted free

iii.
while you check
water courses
keep an eye on

scraps
of drifting
broken bark

on a leaf's
casual swirl
are suspicious

when mud stains
spread
startled

by any
inexplicable
splash

I abide
in fluid darkness
in greeny light

iv.
when you touch
my breasts
nipples harden

when you kiss
a thousand soft mouths
feed

I feel
their spongy assault
their hot suctions

v.
when you lie back
emptied
I stiffen my wings

what comes in the night
finds me vigilant
what crawls in the light

feels my full weight
while you sleep
I open my breast

and drain
my life's blood
into you

bend your head
to the pictured place
direct the blade

from left to right
establish
what we are

PART 3

i.
a hooded bird
stains
every bough

with a slow
intake of breath
a shape subsides

a reflux
sours
my chest

I taste
uncertainty
and dread

ii.

I hear
a woman's voice
in the thin leaves

I hear
a woman's voice
in the sharp seas

the sound a hare makes
in the trap's spike
the sound a bird makes

in the wave's ice
the sound a woman makes
in the dawn's night

iii.

I crawl after you
into the marsh
come upon

a doll's hairless head
a dry, wrinkled skin
sallow and flaked

strings of flesh
on your arms and side
skin bags on your chest

dry hip knobs
stilt legs
brittle knees

I carry you back
your arms
close as a child's

around my neck
lay you softly
in the sand

oh, my love,
your mouth
opens wide

I feel a taut tongue
nipples hard as nails
legs clenched tight

NOTES

The mythology and history of the Kiowas may be read in the following:

Marriott, Alice. *The Ten Grandmothers. Epic of the Kiawas.* (1945)
Momaday, N. Scott. *The Way to Rainy Mountain.* (1976)
Mooney, James. *Calendar History of the Kiowa Indians.* (1979)

Irish Mythology and history may be read in these:

Cross, T.P. and C.H. Slover. *Ancient Irish Tales.* (1936)
Jackson, K.H. *A Celtic Miscellany.* (1951)
Moody, T.W. and F.X. Martin. *The Course of Irish History.* (1967, rev. 1995)

The Boarder

i.

Like the hull of a great liner
the dark building towered above him
windows were portholes in the gloom.

He was led by long hallways
flights of stairs
to rooms so large he felt his littleness
was dazed by the vast space of the Common Room
the coldness of the Refectory
bleak rows of desks in the Study Hall
narrow iron beds in the Dormitory.

Far below, Martin saw
boys parading slowly round the grounds.

ii.

Fr. Brophy stood in the corridor
inspecting them as they passed.
'Head up', he said, 'don't slouch.
Keep your arms to your side, shoulders back'.

In class corrected their speech.
To boys who clamped their teeth
said, 'Speak out. Open your mouth.
Let the sounds out'. When they said

'min' for 'men' or 'pin' for 'pen',
he roared, 'Men, men, men,
pen, pen, pen. Get it right.
You're not in the bogs now'.

Many said, 'Cele*brate*', 'conju*gate*', 'dedi*cate*'.
It exasperated him.
He drilled the correction into them:

'Celebrate', 'conjugate', 'dedicate'.
'Let me hear it'. 'Let me hear it'.

Martin spoke slowly
to avoid being shamed
and shaming where he came from

iii.

The priest inspected them,
hands, nails, ears, neck.
If he found a mark roared,
'Dirty fellow, go out, wash yourself.
There's no place here for pigs.'

In his first talk in the study hall
he said, 'Work hard, pray hard.
That was all God asked
That was all he asked

'Not every boy could be brilliant
not every boy could get First Class Honours
but every boy could do his best.'

They had to put family feeling
away.

Christ asked them
to leave father and mother
and follow Him.

iv.

'You, my dear boys, will have
the inestimable privilege of being
God's anointed.

'There is no greater calling,
no greater gift.

'But the way is not easy.
There is no place, no place in God's holy church
for the boy who takes pleasure in impure thoughts
or impure actions.

'You cannot face Almighty God
on the altar, if your body, temple of the Holy Ghost,
has sinned.'

v.

It was, Martin thought,
a secret society

with rules
he should follow

the Rule of Three
the Rule of Touch
the Rule of Silence

Cleanliness
next to Godliness

vi.

He held up the Book of Don'ts.
'Manners,' he said, 'maketh the man.
Hold your knife and your fork
so that you won't poke the eye
out of your neighbour's head.
Stick your elbows to your side
not into his ribs.'

He angled his arms
and sawed in and out, exaggerating.
The boys laughed.

'Don't slurp your soup.'
He scooped imaginary ladles
sucking, slavering.

'Don't pile your food onto your fork
and never make a fork out of your knife.'
He lowered his head
shovelled in forkful after laden forkful.

'Don't make your gob a cement-mixer.
Keep your mouth shut while you chew.'
He chomped, swilling noisily.
They laughed, uneasily.

The theme was appetite
the inner man
ready to gorge

or that fiercer power
lustful flesh.

vii.
hic haec hoc
hunc hanc hoc

Day after day, week after week
Fr. Murphy drove them through the grammar
round and round
front back
back front.

His rebukes:
the lashing of whips.
His knuckle-strikes:
nails driven in teak.
His thumbprint
branding their ears.

Fear made Martin forget

tear-stained

helpless

viii.

While others walked the garden paths
round and round, three by three
he sought the court's release.

He loved to drive the ball
high and hard
to angle his return
to deaden a shot into the butt
ensuring a point.

He learnt to judge his serve
so that the ball fell close
to the side wall
forcing a finger-tipped riposte.
Some had delicate skills
deceptive, feathery strokes
sudden, quick flicks
a deadly accuracy that flogged
the hard ball
varying direction and pace.

He loved all that
the partnership
the rivalry.

ix.

'God,' Fr. Brophy said,
'would not be fooled.

'He knew they made their natures flow.
They could fool him.
They could not fool God.

'They must be honest with themselves.
They must be manly.

'God is merciful.
He understands
but He is nobody's fool.'

x.
Sometimes hearing a train
coupling, shunting
rumbling slowly off
whistles wailing through the night

Martin let himself think of Ardgillan
blacked-out carriages fleeing through the woods
red sparks rocketing into the dark

his father flagging the train
the engine hissing, spitting
seething at this interruption

the Captain descending
and walking slowly onto the avenue
in a circle of warm light

xi.
A boy ran away

They felt he lacked
the right spirit
and were afraid.

You might know
when someone didn't have it.

Might think you had it
but it could disappear
in a solitary lapse
an impure thought.

xii.
Each day
they moved
one place to the right.

They slid
from place to place
from table to table

to the head table
to shed the skin of words
but Martin's tongue

stuck to the roof of his mouth
while the beast
coiled on without him.

The days slowed.
Through high windows
he watched the advance

of sluggish clouds.
Rain scrabbled
the glass.

The priest waited.
Others talked
yet he could not.
Sentences were journeys
he might not complete
ravined, treacherous.

Suspected of stubborn silence
of proud refusal
his suitability in question.

He forced words out
did enough
for the beast to carry him.

xiii.

'Called upon to do this, do that, Hamlet is unsure. A spirit charges him with a great responsibility. But he doesn't feel up to it. He thinks prevarication is an option, a refuge. He can live in uncertainty, biding his time.

But is it a manageable choice? Is it morally justified? Can pretence, a form of lying, be an acceptable mode of behaviour? Is it workable?'

Fr. Monahan gazed calmly at them
waiting.

Could a man live like that
pretending to be what he was not?

xiv.

Martin wrote for him:

'A late storm toppled a tree. For months it lay, torn from the gaping soil. Then they tackled it. Big enough to handle small axe and light sledge while his father used the heavy blade and drove wedges hard into bursting, splintering cracks. Together. Arms, backs, shoulders, legs taking the strain. Matching strength to task. A day's work. A ringing, clanging, cloudless day.

Mishits made wedge-heads spark and tingles judder through hands and arms. His father cursed. They laughed, wiping sweat from the sockets of their eyes. This year he had stood over the split half taking it on. His father said, "That's it, son, that'll do." They piled logs beside the horse. Sawing another day's work.'

xv.

The weather put them under siege.
Clouds swept in from the hills.
Rain drenched the courts.
Fog seeped into the hallways.

They sat in the Common Room
talking in groups
or playing cards.

There were no papers
no magazines
no radio.

Released
padded back and forth
in the covered walk.

xvi.

Fr Brophy placed the Host in his mouth
and enunciated slowly
and deliberately

HOC EST ENIM CORPUS MEUM.

Martin bowed his head
and heard the bell's gentle call.

All the chapel lights were on
row upon row of white candles
on each side of the tabernacle
tulips pure and erect around the Virgin's statue.

Feast of the Immaculate Conception.

The smell of incense
filtered slowly
back to the benches.

The entire school sang the plain chant
wave after wave of song
lifting towards the altar.

Behind them
deep, triumphant tones
soared from the harmonium.

xvii.

It would be easier
if they never went home.

Then nothing could upset
the way they lived.

Nothing could crack
the mould to which they clung.

The day's routine
the bell's control.

Fr. Brophy warned them
against the snares of the world.
Its tinsel charms
its craving for flesh.

No one ever talked of home
but when it was time to go
Martin felt a lightness.
The ice of routine
melting in memory.

Nothing prepared him
for her faded hair
her slight form.

His father's wordlessness.
The gap between what had been
and what now was.

As though he had come
from a distant, incomprehensible place.

He walked the woods
looked at the grey sea
listened to the song
of a solitary bird.

xviii.
Met a girl from the Black Hills
helpless as he was
wordless as he was.

Against wall, door, tree
thrusting, panting, desperate, hurrying
in case someone might see.

They returned
time after time.

Then he had to go back.

xix.
Martin knew he should place himself
in the priest's hands

but was on guard
suspicious of silky persuasion

casual questions
parried
with casual replies

bad thoughts?
touch?

knowing the ordeal
would come again

what had been said
must not be unsaid

xx.

Sometimes a boy would not be where he should be
a vacant place in chapel
a silence at roll-call.
'Gone to the infirmary.'

A place no one talked about
where Martin sweated and burned.
Brother changed his sheets
brought fresh pajamas.

Would he be sent home?
If he had to leave
this is how it would be.

Under a cloud
Silence
Disappointment
Shame.

xxi.

A dream-place
a fire in the grate
his clothes folded away
a tray with boiled eggs and toast
on a linen cloth.
Unlike their long corridors
and cold linoleum
expectant teachers
the bell's commands
the Director seizing his wrist
asking if he'd given in to bad thoughts.

Comforting thoughts
reachings, touchings
tears of tenderness.

A dream-place
immune to bells
unanswerable.

xxii.
Before the bellman
clanged them up
Martin lowered himself
to the floor.

Begged forgiveness
sought protection
against temptation.

Gutted prayer books
and Saints's Lives
for aspirations
and short prayers
that he could summon
to his aid.

Fortified himself
with scapulars
and holy medals.

xxiii.
The priest questioned him
persistently.

How many times
did he give in to bad thoughts?
How often did he touch himself?

He must not persist
in this foul practice.

He would never be any good.

He could not stand at the altar
taking the sacred body and blood of Christ
into his hands.

How could he forgive sin
if he himself were ensnared?

He confessed repeatedly.
Bad thoughts.
Excitement of the flesh.

Unable to say how much was deliberate
how much not his fault.

xxiv.
Beset with desire
a force he could not stem.
Out of the world
yet caught in its slime.
Smell like the reek
of steeping rags.

xxv.
They would hear music
and imagine Fr. Brophy in his great cloak
sitting alone in the Common Room
listening with stiff face
to *Orpheus in the Underworld*
Tannhäuser
the *Unfinished Symphony*
the *1912 Overture*
Finlandia.
Sometimes after study
they sat in a circle
listening with him.

As the sounds filled the room
Martin wanted to shout

to clench fists above his head

to pound on wood.

His skin crawled.

Afterwards
unable to sleep
his hand cradled flesh.

xxvi.
He wrote again for Fr. Monahan:

'They cut the tips off. First the little one halfway from
the half-moon.
They kept at it tip after tip until all were shortened.

But the more they cut the more the fingers numbly resisted.

The process went on. The gleaming instrument exact and perfect
for skin and bone. But the blood held, the veins renewed.'

xxvii.
They prayed together
walked together in threes
kept silence together.

He did not tell lies
did not steal
did not use bad words.

Imitated others
their pious demeanour
coming back from the altar.

Their rapt faces
raised
at each Station of the Cross.

They guarded their tongues

against mean words.
So did he.

Each day left a portion of sweet
for the Child Jesus.
So did he.

xxviii.

'Now, like a good lad,
stand up there till we see
have you lost or gained.'

Stripped for the scales
fear made his shorts
stick to him.

'Shoulders back,
arms by your side.'

Fr. Doc bent close
to see the numbers
his ear a stethoscope
at the groin's ferment.

Drops trickled on Martin's neck.
His legs shook.

'And how is young Mikey today?

Ah!' reaching inside the vent,
'big as a turkey's head.

But not as big as old Mikey.
This rod,
this staff,
this discipline.'

From inside the folds of the soutane
he raised
the gross distended flesh.

'Now, like a good lad.'

xxix.
They faced each other again.

The priest held his wrist
while he questioned.

Martin kept calm.
He knew his part
expected to be human
to fall
to rise again
manfully.

The script his to write
so many times for this
so many times for that.

Ejaculation.
Prayer.
The good man fell.
He could fall
must rise again.

All he had to do was say it
plan it
get the pace right.

xxx.
In the potato shed,
on old sacks,
in an odour of mould

assailed,
unassuaged.

No one talked of home.
Out of the world,
spared its trashy lures.

His winter bird
high in the fir

Singing
as though in mating time

In cool dawn
in yielding dark.

xxxi.
At morning mass
the Director evoked a presence
disturbing the soul,
feeding with evil thoughts,
an insidious force
coursing through all things
battening on mind and flesh.
The day of the Retreat moved with dull uncertainty
he walked in silence from the covered walk
to the handball alley
from the handball alley to the stone wall
that shut out the world.

Others paraded silently along the narrow paths
that bordered on the glasshouse
or framed flower beds and apple trees.

No matter where he walked
No matter what he thought
No matter how he prayed
his mind could not respond
to the change that had come inside him.

He saw himself at a distance
walking the grounds
kneeling in chapel
head bowed in an attitude of prayer
his mind lapsed
his body wearied.

xxxii.
It was his last essay:

'Fitting the frame over the shaven skull the Director lowered the point, drilled a tiny opening into the seam. A fine dust spread under the beam of light. Again the instrument made a minute aperture. Finally, there were five points of release.

After the initial prick, the involuntary clench, no pain. Instead, a compacting against the cold steel. Each time the instrument made its fine revolutions tissue and bone held. The dust spread its fantail of light.'

xxxiii.
he had fitted in
left the woods
left the shore

grey cement, dull stone
dull stone, grey cement
beds, corridors, desks

his mind shrank
his tongue
sank in its bed.

Ardgillan

High and low
these are my woods:
the wild frontier
where I move like a fox
sniffing the air;
song-havens for thrush and finch,
trails that spiral
to pond and pleasure ground.

When they stretch at their ease
beneath the yew,
the topping and tailing done,
what can I find but peace?

When they amble along in May or June
tapers touching the long grass,
cattle chewing the cud,
what can I feel but ease?

When we go to the shore
for a basin of brine
to bathe my knee
what can I know but love?

When she pulls me along to early Mass,
the sea in shrouds,
the wall a mortuary door
what can I be but innocent?

When I clamor and cry
to dig for clams
on a freezing night
what am I but a spoiled brat?

I could go on
but the scenes give way
black smoke pours to the old nests
the chimney roars,
sparks assault the sky.

He is stevedore, stoker, fire god.
She is wailing, praying, doom-filled.
I am racing out
to cower in the dell.

It is God's rage and wrath.
Anger, grief, my in-between fear.

Photographs

Formal studio-work, decorative props.
A seated, wellmade, handsome man.
A well-dressed woman standing by his side
fingers touching his left shoulder.
The pose assigned. Attitudes in place.
Nothing flares from those delicate tips.
Those shoulders stiff as standing stones.
No one smiles in these family scenes.

I'm glum and pudgy-faced, with curly hair.
She is just as stolid, ringleted, beautiful,
the child that broke their hearts. Nor does
the older boy, face beginning its shape,
oblige the dicky-bird. We've come to town
for the yearly trial at Lafayettes. The man
in black covers his head with sackcloth
and brings the shutter down like a guillotine.

Where did it go wrong? I was too young
to comprehend. The child's death in Mary's month.
Grief, I was told, held the house in its dark claw.
Her framed photograph hung in the parlour,
unsmiling, tinted, enlarged. Her solemnity
mirrored the processional's pained finality.
Like the rest of us in these cold capturings.
Her unspoken name part of a serious stillness.

Why did the woman take to prayer
as some to drink? One day Wylie's pony and trap
clanked onto the avenue and stopped outside.
The statues stood like bare-faced refugees,
Joseph in brown, Mary in blue and white,
the child's arms outstretched in numb appeal.
Unwelcome signs from that day forth
of our fractured insufficiency.

She made an altar in our room, draped white lace
over bald heads, filled vases with flowers,
daisies, bluebells, anemone, honeysuckle.
Sang hymns about the house. A breathless, gentle woman
whose health I undermined forcing my way,
large as life. A genial man who erupted
into rage, warp-spasm, transfiguration.
I too would down the ox with a mad thump.

When I asked what she was like as a girl
he said, 'she followed me everywhere.'
Love? Helplessness? Did he treat her well?
I have these inexpressive photographs
and a postcard from the West Indies.
Mother and child. Not given to words
or shows of feeling. You can fill rooms
with fury and love those in the eye.

Her passion for piety put me off –
prayer leaflets, ejaculations, novenas,
the Nine Fridays dragging through the year,
one sure to be missed, then the strain
beginning again. I suffered shiny medals pinned
to my braces, scapulars coiled about
my neck in sweaty embarrassment.
Choked on the outrageous Nicene Creed.

Preferred being and doing. Wheeled
the barrow from the dung-heap to the garden
where he forked the hot pads along the dry bottoms,
planted the seed one by one, heaped
the coverlet of warm clay. A tight, dynamic
world. His and mine. I witnessed green shoots rising
all along the line, saw how rhubarb sprang to life
in the dark womb of the half-barrel.

She had other tunes, the bird in a gilded cage,
it was only a beautiful picture in a beautiful
golden frame. My heart was a weeping statue
when her spectral voice filtered through the rooms.
I put the hen to sleep with a gentle motion.
As the field-mouse crept closer to the house
Hector sent a sharp reply to the dell vixen,
jackdaws closed eyes in the sleepy smoke.

Unhappiness wired itself about my bones.
Untamed, uncouth, in cutaway clothes, I prowled
the two estates, the dog sniffing and fierce, rabbits
racing for briar and burrow, a hare erect,
poised, sure of herself, softly luminous.
In May took my place beneath the gaudy signs,
hymns dragging me from one end of the street to the other,
a good, imperfect christian from Borneo.

A stillness here, the figures trapped
in a silence too deep for words. Nothing
transferred. They left scant evidence
of who they were or what they came from.
A tale of an Ascendancy mismatch
traced in her elegance and good taste.
That beautiful embroidered shawl, that grace.
Jutland, the Dardanelles, Nerissa. His.

They never talked of the past. I have
these studio photographs, a wooden
horse, figures posed, standing, seated,
a ringleted girl, two soft-faced boys,
pasty flesh unmarked, unscored as yet
with flats and sharps. The good life? A life
off-key. I can sing of woods and shore,
not of my stiff, unyielding, handsome people.

Yet they worked for me, bruised though I was
in mind and spirit, troubled from the start.
They kept on and kept me on
from day to day, from year to silent year.
What I am they helped to bring about,
provided the means, did without,
put it up to me. In turn I stuck with it,
one damaging, helpful school after another.

And now, my children out on their own,
I rub these worn replicas, remembering.
The last time I saw him he was standing
in Dublin Street in the old blue faded gaberdine
waving me off to Oregon. The last time
I saw her she wrinkled her nose at death's
bad taste. Pictures, confusions,
memories, still lives, uncertain loves.

Bogieman

Ned Daly takes me on his lap,
hoops his arms about me,
carries me off through strange smells –
hayseed, sour milk, tobacco, paraffin –
to sway and rumble down the avenue.
Rims and hooves fling music right
and left to oak and sycamore.

We clank across the railway lines,
roll into the muffled silence of the sea fields,
sink in fresh grass and sandy soil.

A hundred cocks are waiting just for this,
watchtowers circled by gulls,
where crows have pecked and mice bedded,
where cliff hares raced.
Invisible, mysterious in sea-mist,
each in a circle of dream, self-absorbed, imagining.

Waves lap the rocks at Longleg,
lair of the reef-hags whose sunken eyes
know deadly combat under waves.
Goods trains shunt inside their heads
with stone and gravel brought from Milverton,
cars with beasts blowing through the slats,
eyes white, moonlit, aghast.

All this we crank,
soliloquies to the whispering seas.
The dreamy yield, the slow ascent,
and that moment when the weight of seasoned grass
eases the platform down on the riveted frame.

In those days, in that place

On Sunday afternoons we would sit outside
by the public road, fifty yards from home.
Ready for anything: Numidians, Chinese hulks,
Duffy's caravans in cavalcade; lions, tigers,
trapeze artistes, cyclists pedalling on their hands,
stiltmen walking with God above the telegraph wires.

Sometimes we had a yacht race off Skerries,
angelwings flitting about the buoys.
We never knew who won or if winning
was in anybody's mind, so gauzy their pace.
Enough just to be serene. From where we sat
the ocean was a glaze they floated on,
cotton motes, thistledown. Why think
of being first or last? The middle
might be best, motion gauged by slow drift,
twinkling companions in a milky way.

Winter gales bent trees in two,
reclaimed roads, smashed walls,
kept us at bay, dredgers of roads
where ships shuddered and died.
Tellers of old tales, revivalists,
we sank our heads in the sands.

In summer emerged again to see
pilgrims wading slowly through iodined air,
filling their lungs. Mothers exposing
their babies' heads to the wind-balm
and sun-chrism of this coast.

A bee mumbles in a grassy maze,
a ladybird feels the line across my palm,
a seabreeze softly stirs,
while on a whitened bough a chaffinch
sings the beauty of then and now

Slow Learner

We lived so far from town I did
not go to school for years,
truant of woods and shore.

I knew the ways of birds,
could track the rabbit and the fox,
guarded the hens against the hawk.

When goats were born I raised
them as my own, when pups were drowned
I mourned, but loved the one we saved.

I got no marks at school for flinging sticks,
could neither read nor write, so late
to class the Catechism was my ABC.

Christ sat upon the mat. Morality was strange:
commandments, mysteries, big sins, little sins.
I was a rabbit trapped within the furze.

I reared away from priestly bit and ban.
I shied from sin. What I knew best
was climbing slowly through dreamy firs

until I hung above a swaying world,
could see the castle turning on its hill,
could feel the ocean roll towards Rockabill.

Stone Games

Remember how we played with stones,
made cock-shots out of tins,
propped them on rocks, took turns
to send a tin-can rattling from its throne;

Or how we endlessly pursued
the art of skimming stones, believing
if we chose a certain shape, held
it right and sent it on a level course
that it would replicate its flying feet?

Looking back, I marvel how persistently
we played this game; your seven year lead
gave you the edge, which egged me on –
bend closer to the strand, relax,

The art of skimming stones does not
depend on strength alone, there is an ease,
a measuring of the self with sea and strand,
a nonchalance infusing hand and mind.

We had another game: a stone
of any shape flung high, then
as it faltered, turned and fell, we tried
to intercept its quickening plunge.

We took failure in our stride
and ever since I've sought
satisfaction in work being done, done right,
and not in praise or honour to be won.

Two Estates

An iron gate between the two estates.
Beyond games of hide and seek, her slow run.
I let her find me, our catch-as-catch can.

She propped her back against a fallen stump.
Sometimes I wandered off, never too far
lest sadness come upon her unawares.

Sometimes just silence. Sometimes eloquent
with song: the wind that shakes the barley,
the ash grove, the bird in a gilded cage.

Once upon a time she walked through this wood
carrying home-made bread, or scones,
delaying to pick bluebells, or violets,

To loop a daisy-chain, her wicker basket
topped with apples, hazel nuts, trailing flowers,
red cloak here and there between the trees.

Airs and graciousness, stories, poems, songs.
The postman's gate, with sheets of black tin
riveted to the bars, opened on pleasure ground.

The Return

I sit by the pond
in the spell of ripple and fly

stand under trees
in the poignancy of leaves

lie offshore
in the fluency of stems

feel the stone's tremor
in the drain of waves

see pitch and stress
in the spider's web

find conclusions
in a grain of sand

discover an air
coldly sufficient

reliable
as the avenue of yew

The Undergraduate

i.

A smell of burning leaves in the Green,
but scattered remnants lift and twirl beside the pond
as Martin hurries towards Earlsfort Terrace.
When he pushes through the double doors
noise assaults him, shouts, laughter,
footsteps clattering on black and white tiles.
Students are hurrying to classes,
ascending the stairs at either side.

A tall figure in black with a bald head
moves intently about,
singling out individual students.
Already questioned – name, place, school, subject –
Martin avoids the piercing blue eyes,
the womanish hands.
He'd had enough of that.

In a chalk-stained old gown
draped from his thin shoulders,
in a mournful voice the professor
paraphrases, explains hard words,
gives biographical information,
reads *Midsummer Night Madness* in a variety of voices,
speaks of 'Moltin's' *Paradise Lost.*
He strolls in the valleys of tradition,
at ease with what he knows.
Aloof in the corridors,
unapproachable.

ii.

Extrovert, mannered, well-spoken, theatrical.
A woman lecturer at the English Lit.
spoke of 'we literary people.'

She had been seen in a red roadster with Kate O'Brien,
in Bewleys with Mary Lavin.

Once on a dusty morning
produced the white rabbits of imagination,
declaiming lines, pausing to comment,
advancing, harking back,
following the repetitions.

Queens young, fair,
dust in Helen's eyes,
pain, loss.

Infused with light
on a dusty morning,
in an old classroom,
white rabbits, white doves,
humanity's sad music.

iii.

One man had a professional air.
About him too legend grew.
His arrest by the Special Branch:
heavy footsteps on the stairs,
his class continuing,
they march in, ask his name,
take him off to internment;
he and Val Iremonger
had staged a protest at the Abbey,
had been thrown out.
It was said he'd had a fight in London with Paddy Kavanagh.
It was said he'd given a shed in Rathmines
where the IRA shackled a man.
It was said he was at odds with the Administration
for his liberal views.

He lingered after tutorials
to talk and share cigarettes,
spoke of writers he knew,
wrote for *The Bell*,
appeared on platforms with Seán O'Faoláin,
argued for the release of Casement Diaries.

He plotted the growth of an indigenous literature.
Writers identified Irish issues,
drew on native sources,
reflected life and character,
gave the lie to the simian lip.

Map-maker, pioneer,
drawing out of the past
achievements
played down in standard histories.

iv.

On Saturday afternoons
Martin sat at the back of the shabby theatre
in the smell of dust and stale air.
From a side alcove a few musicians
evoked a finer age – Mozart, Beethoven, Bach.
On stage – Sheridan, Wilde, Shakespeare, Chekhov –
drawing rooms, upperclass life,
women in full gowns, shoulders creamy under the light,
men in elegant trousers, fine waistcoats, cravats,
a language unlike any he had heard.
A sense of performance,
expansive gestures, expressive speech.
It was, he thought, the theatre's gift,
to create a fiction, to draw him in.
Drab seats, dull walls, stale smells did not matter.
Once the curtain rose,
the first movement and gesture enacted,
the performance possessed him.

v.

It began quietly.
He asked her to dance
and they moved slowly around the hall.
Putting him at ease
with talk of a friend's birthday party.

They danced again.
He had a sense of warmth,
vivacity, natural beauty.

Outside the sea he had always known
rose about the islands and harbour,
Rockabill spread its light,
the Mountains of Mourne held their ground.

They began to meet once a week.
Would go to a cafe,
he uncertain at first,
stumbling over words,
grateful that she talked.

Choosing a film they emerge
into a city already beginning to glow,
shop windows filling with light,
street lamps crowned above their heads,
buses bright as ocean liners.

vi.

Once a week they washed bottles,
sitting each side of the tub,
jabbing the wire brush briskly into each,
rinsing, scouring old labels off,
turning the bottles to drain.
Behind the counter he fumbled over change,
unable to talk of crops, fairs,

heifers, lambing, the price of seed.
Never asked to help when the bar was full,
voices shouting for drinks,
long orders he couldn't remember,
red faces, cigarette smoke thick in the air,
plug tobacco stinging his eyes,
corks pulled, pints filled,
the head rising, scooped, topped again.
Not worth a curse, his father knew, at hanging a gate,
swinging a scythe, fixing tackle.

vii.

From the Black Hills, Man O'War, Knockbrack,
from Tubbersool, Stamullen, Gormanstown,
they came on bicycles,
lights bobbing through the blackness.
Others walked from Balrothery, Blackhall, the Glebe,
guided by houses, clumps of trees,
drawn by thumping music, coloured lights,
excited voices, the swirl of anonymous flesh,
the off-chance of sex.

The hall fills,
men on one side,
women on the other,
Tom Hagan beaming on stage,
butcher by day, bandsman at night,
the keys of his piano accordion
sparkling under his hands, sides
ablaze under the arcs,
playing the latest tunes.

'I hear you're at the uni.'
'Mmm.'
'What's it like?'
'It's alright.'

It couldn't be explained:
the walk through the Green,
theatres, tutorials,
ideas held to see if they could be upheld,
days without constraint.
He sang in the dance to avoid speech,
saw his face in the wall's mirror,
foolish, glistening, out of place.

viii.

He had exchanged one kind of asceticism for another.
Every evening in his room,
read through *Paradise Lost*, the *Prelude*,
The Faerie Queene, 'The Scholar Gypsy',
The Odyssey, *Tasso*, *The Decameron*, Dante,
The Magic Mountain, *The Castle*,
gobbling like a goose at a basin of grain,

Discovered the structure of 'Lycidas',
the line's freedom in Arnold,
the real presences in Browning.
From the dancefloor's barren rounds
to the waltz of the imagination,
night after night, burrowing, taking deep breaths,
like a runner getting his second wind,
a singer leaning back on a column of air,
homemade shelves filling like an estuary.

ix.

High in the gods, on the packed benches,
straining to see the bright patch,
figures weaving, floating,
lifted in flight, soaring, the music
fused with each step, the girl
on her toes, a butterfly flitting along,
arms like wings, face a serene mask,

seemingly sexless but the shapes assembling,
starkly defined, muscular calves, thighs, crotch,
intensity, male hands, female response,
leaning together, parting, intent,
still joined, in full passion,
returning, a swoon of feeling.
So graceful, more beautiful
than anything he had imagined.
Season after season, *Swan Lake, Coppelia, Everyman.*

Never had he known such rapture,
remote drama of body and spirit,
transcending the litter of life;
effortless, restrained unrestrained expression,
concentration in a lit space,
feeling illuminated,
so that, reality mimimised, excluded,
the dancers exposed feeling,
desire, loss, waste, tragic gaiety.

x.

They met laughing on Nelson's Pillar,
went to the zoo where she clapped her hands
in merriment before the monkey's cage;
were silenced by the epitaph in St. Patrick's Cathedral;
she felt the woman's breast in St. Michan's,
he shook hands with the crusader.
They caught productions in the old Abbey.
Making the city theirs,
museums, galleries, river vistas
discovered together, built into them.

On St.Patrick's Day or Easter Monday
they danced at the Crystal Ballroom,
to favourite songs,
'Mona Lisa','Put another nickle in',

'The Tennessee Waltz', 'Buttons and Bows'.
They could enter the liveliness,
lost in the rhythms
she on her mettle,
he taken out of himself.
They kept their romance secret.
In a circle of privacy
protected what they had,
perfecting it.

xi.

Fresh from Cambridge, fresh-faced, plump, preening,
scholarship poured from the new lecturer
in eloquent periods, multiple allusions.

Piers Plowman, its field of folk,
reflected an entire society,
connected with Dante, Boethius, Chaucer,
predated Elizabethan individualism.
Week after week the lectures worked the issues,
the history of manuscripts, the editions.

What they were given exceeded
what they might be expected to know.
Behind his approach the implication
that someone here
might strap on the satchel of scholarship.

In this time, this place, this mastery,
next time, in another place, one of them
might enter the succession.

xii.

In spring and summer they went to Howth Head,
lying in bracken and fern,
seagulls circling close to the cliffs.
No day was too long,

together, one with the racing clouds
the skylark in its spiral of song,
the breeze riffling the long grass,
the rabbit nibbling at the cliff's edge.

They loved the bus journey out from the city,
the old tram lurching and rattling to the top,
the brief walk to the summit,
the first sight of the sea,
stretching out and out far as they could see,
the walk down the goat paths,
finding a private place,
arranging the picnic things,
the long day ahead, the hours, free, alone.

Even the walk back to the late tram,
bodies drugged with sea-air,
the slow welling of feeling, the sharing of food,
holding hands, conclusion in the west,

xiii.
The American professor laid it on the line.
Night and Morning, a conflict faced,
repression harrowing the soul
now taking a stand inside the Church,
invoking a time when reason was respected,
saying I will not be put down.

The Great Hunger, the repressed life,
barrenness amid fields of growth,
his seed cast in the ashes,
imagination repossessing,
transcending failure.

Seán O'Faoláin took on the Paudeens,
politicians, the Jansenist church.
It was the job of the artist to bear witness,
to criticise, let ideas in.

Steady, subtle, learned,
uncompromising,
beyond sentiment,
the respect of rigour.

xiv.
Ardgillan strand was theirs.
He liked to be first,
to see her appear at the water's edge,
surf spuming, the old bicycle
laden with food, utensils, plates,
a package strapped to the carrier,
her face alight, legs pumping against the sand.
He could hardly speak, reaching out for the bike,
helping to carry their lunch to the flat rocks.
Swimming together, diving from a favourite spot,
afraid to touch her, so almost naked.
The sting of salt, the tingling wave,
a temptation accepted, indulged, not spoken about.
They lacked words for strong feelings,
too shy to mention them,
had never heard the language of desire,
did not know what to expect, what might be normal.

He had known desire as an irrepressible force,
respecting no place, no occasion,
as liable to occur in class or church,
in conversation, in reading,
the kiss on the page compelling as a fever,
repressed, fought against, checked,
unstoppable, coming again and again.
No amassing of grace, no clerical injunctions,
nothing, nothing, could put an end to it.

The risks were chosen now, part of them.
Long days, the sea turning, glistening,
the rocks warming as the day advanced,

air making them ravenous,
the tea's rich smell on the primus,
lettuce, hard boiled eggs, cold ham,
homemade brown bread, salt, pickles,
her apple tart so richly sugared,
the juice dribbled over their chins.

Laughter, completion, fullness, contentment holding
as the sun went back behind the cliffs,
the rooks flew to the Ladies Stairs
and darkness folded the demesne.

xv.
In the end it happened.
Leeson Street transformed,
a cartwheel of milky light spilling between the houses.
Afterwards they could no longer resist.
Once at his insistence expressed contrition
for all their sins, for the offence.
He was filled with shame
at bringing in sin's sour note.
In confession he hated the questioning,
'was she a married woman?'
'did you withdraw?',
'will you promise not to do it again?'
In rage at the absurdity he would promise,
trying to convince himself he would do better.
Even when he did any sign of her need
made him yield in love, in tenderness.

All that spring and summer he struggled,
confessed, promised, lapsed, hating
the institution that made no allowances
for pods bursting,
birds soaring, water pouring.

How could he separate the beat in the blood,
her bones numbered beneath his hands,
all her joints, all the tender tension
of her vertebrae, the stretched drum of her chest,
the knobs of her shoulders, the plates of her knee?
When he held her now he felt all at once.
She was as real, as fluid, as envisioned as stained glass.
The slightest contact, hand in his,
thigh brushing, bright glance, laughter,
swept scruple aside,
any of these made her flesh and spirit manifest.

It was a miracle of flesh and flesh,
body triumphant, glorious senses,
like music, pure idea, pure sensation, dance,
more absolute than cherubim
and seraphim could trumpet forth.
Beyond the calculations of morality,
the reproach of class, the fear of priest.

They struggled in its surge, frightened,
counted days,
tried not to meet
but since she only had one day off,
had to meet, succumbed,
counted in anxiety and misery.

He no longer studied,
no longer went to the library,
walked sometimes by the canal
in dull, repetitive assessment,
knowing there was no way out.

He could no longer confess,
would not submit to its degradation,
its belittlement.

xvi.
Throughout the long summer students
prepared for the final examination.

He knew what he had to do
but his heart was not in it.
Others joked about making novenas,
praying to favourite saints.

He could not do it.
He owed Him that much.